EDGE
BOOKS™

BIZARRE THINGS
WE'VE CALLED
MEDICINE

BY ALICIA KLEPEIS

Consultant:
Marjorie J. Hogan, MD
University of Minnesota
and Hennepin County Medical Center
Associate Professor of Pediatrics and Pediatrician

CAPSTONE PRESS
a capstone imprint

Edge Books are published by Capstone Press,
1710 Roe Crest Drive, North Mankato, Minnesota 56003
www.capstonepub.com

Library of Congress Cataloging-in-Publication Data
Cataloging-in-Publication data is on file with the Library of Congress.
ISBN 978-1-4914-4266-1 (library binding)
ISBN 978-1-4914-4342-2 (paperback)
ISBN 978-1-4914-4322-4 (eBook PDF)

Developed and Produced by Focus Strategic Communications, Inc.
  Adrianna Edwards: project manager
  Ron Edwards: editor
  Rob Scanlan: designer and compositor
  Mary Rose MacLachlan: media researcher
  Francine Geraci: copy editor and proofreader
  Wendy Scavuzzo: fact checker

Photo Credits
Alamy: Heritage Image Partnership Ltd, cover, Interfoto, 19, Paris Pierce, 20; Bridgeman Images: Egyptian National Library, Cairo, Egypt, 7; Copyright 1999 by Oak Ridge Associated Universities, 11; Copyright 2011 by Canadian Medical Association, 26; Corbis: National Geographic Creative, 16; Getty Images: DEA/D. Dagli Orti, 28, Heritage Images/History of Advertising Trust, 27, Leemage, 18, Oliver Strewe, 25; Library of Congress, 15; Newscom: Custom Medical Stock Photo/EP Concepts, 14, Prisma, 8; Science Source: Mona Lisa Production/Thierry Berrod, 23, Sam Ogden, 9; Shutterstock: aaltair, 22, Alon Brik, 24, BMCL, 6 (left), Fotokvadrat, 5, Johan Swanepoel, 4, Kruglov_Orda, 13, Rob Byron, 12, Torwaiphoto, 17, Vinne, 29, Volosina, 6 (right); Wikimedia: Quibik, 10, Rakesh Ahuja, MD, 21

Design Elements by Shutterstock

Printed in the United States of America in North Mankato, Minnesota.
042015   008823CGF15

TABLE OF CONTENTS

WACKY MEDICAL REMEDIES

Got a wart on your hand or foot? Try cutting off an eel's head and rubbing its blood over the wart. Is a nasty cold getting you down? One Roman remedy was to drink a jaguar's urine. Not something you are likely to find at the drug store! Does a member of your family wet the bed? Ancient Egyptians wore a bag of mouse bones around the neck to cure bedwetting.

The flesh of the honeycomb moray eel contains poisons that can kill a predator who eats it.

Throughout history doctors have prescribed some bizarre treatments for their patients. And people actually tried them!

BIZARRE FACT

The Ancient Romans treated **epilepsy** with the blood of gladiators. They believed this blood contained the essence of life.

epilepsy—an illness that causes people to have blackouts or convulsions

CHAPTER 1
HEADACHES AND TOOTHACHES

a human brain

Do walnuts look like brains?

Headaches and toothaches are not new ailments. Long ago there were no drug stores to go to for relief from these aches. People came up with their own, rather odd, remedies.

Headache treatments were often bizarre. The Ancient Romans thought eating walnuts would cure headaches. Why? Walnuts look like little brains. Other Romans used electric eels to cure headaches. The electric shocks from the eels were supposed to stun the patient's brain. This would numb the headache.

In the Middle Ages people had other headache cures. One cure was to place three small stones from the stomachs of baby swallows in a pouch. Then the pouch was placed on the patient's head. This headache cure was also supposed to work for eye pain. An Arabian headache remedy at this time was to tie a dead mole to the patient's head.

A doctor examines a patient in this Arabian drawing from the 1300s.

A Hole in the Head

An extreme headache remedy was to drill a hole in the patient's skull. This was called **trepanning**. People in Ancient Greece, Rome, Egypt, and China treated headaches this way. Some healers used a sharp stone to scrape away the bone. Others drilled tiny, circular holes in the patient's skull. Then they pulled out the piece of skull. Ouch!

This painting shows trepanning in Spain during the 1500s.

trepanning—making a hole in a patient's skull, as with a hole saw called a trepan

A surgeon performs brain surgery using a video camera.

Today's brain surgeons use video cameras. Growths deep inside the brain can be removed with only a tiny cut in the patient's head.

BIZARRE FACT

In 1965 a Dutch medical student named Bart Huges drilled a hole in his own head. He performed the operation himself, believing it would expand his consciousness. Huges survived, but he was never able to prove his theory.

Toothache Cures

Toothaches were a common problem before people brushed and flossed regularly. Sore teeth often got pulled out. Ancient Egyptians put a dead mouse on a painful tooth to ease the pain. Perhaps the disgusting practice distracted the sufferer from his pain.

In Wales long ago people thought toothaches were caused by "tooth worms." They would hold a burning candle close to the sore tooth. Then they would put a bowl of cold water under the candle. They thought the worms would try to escape the candle's heat. Then the tooth worms would drop into the water.

A dentist treats a patient for "tooth worms" in this drawing from the 1300s.

TOOTHPASTE THROUGH TIME

Toothpaste has been around for more than 6,000 years. An ancient Chinese toothpaste was made of crushed twigs, bones, and flower petals. The Greeks wanted a toothpaste that was more gritty. So they added oyster shells. The Romans' toothpaste contained bark and powdered charcoal to fight bad breath.

Other toothpastes have contained ashes, powdered ox hooves, or burnt eggshells. But a toothpaste called Doramad from the 1940s was actually harmful. Why? It contained radioactive material. People did not know back then that it could cause cancer.

CHAPTER 2
REVOLTING REMEDIES

Some Ancient Romans thought urine was a miracle cure-all. The writer Cato recommended drinking the urine of people who ate lots of cabbage. He even suggested washing babies in this cabbage-y pee. Some folks today still think drinking urine is good for their health. They believe it can help ward off colds, sore throats, and other illnesses. Pee soup, anyone?

Bottoms up?

Tummy Troubles

Through the ages people have suffered from **constipation**. Some doctors in the 1800s gave patients mercury pills to get things moving. They did not know that mercury is poisonous. American doctor John Kellogg recommended yogurt **enemas**. He thought that squirting yogurt up a patient's bottom would help loosen things up!

A doctor holds an enema syringe.

BIZARRE FACT

In the 1920s a German scientist used coffee enemas to try to treat some illnesses. Today some people still use coffee enemas. But there is no proof that they have any health benefits. However, lemon juice, apple cider vinegar, and chamomile tea enemas could help with constipation.

constipation—difficulty having a bowel movement
enema—an injection of fluid that causes a bowel movement

Bloodletting

People once thought many illnesses came from having bad blood, or too much blood. The solution was to get rid of some. **Bloodletting** was common throughout history. At first sharp stones were used to bleed patients. Later doctors used sharp instruments.

Bloodletting did not cure anything. After all, people die if they lose too much blood. But this practice was used for thousands of years to treat headaches, sore throats, and tons of other health problems. Perhaps people felt better just because they believed the treatment would work.

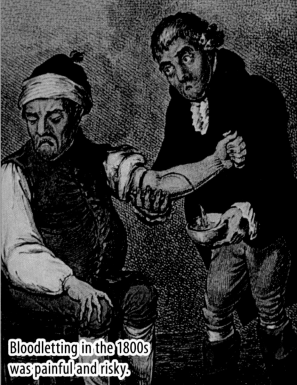

Bloodletting in the 1800s was painful and risky.

BIZARRE FACT

Barbers used to bleed people for medical purposes. They also pulled sore teeth. The red-and-white pole that stood in front of barber shops was a symbol for blood and bandages.

Had it not been for bloodletting, George Washington might have survived his final illness.

THE DEATH OF GEORGE WASHINGTON

It was a cold winter day in 1799. George Washington returned home from a horse ride. He had a sore throat. His condition got worse over the next couple of days. Finally he could not swallow at all. He asked his doctors to bleed him, thinking it would make him feel better.

On Washington's last day of life his doctors bled him a lot. They drained almost half the blood from his body. Washington died later that same day.

bloodletting—the act of letting out blood by opening a vein

15

CHAPTER 3

MAKING THE CUT

This drawing shows a modern artist's idea of a doctor treating a patient in Ancient Egypt.

Doctors in Ancient Egypt performed many types of surgeries. They knew how to treat dislocated legs and arms. They also **cauterized** wounds to stop bleeding and prevent infection. Doctors during the Middle Ages also treated wounds this way. But surgery was risky.

Anesthesia

Alcohol was the earliest form of **anesthesia**. Then came opium, which comes from poppies. In the 1800s ether, chloroform, and morphine were used to help reduce pain.

Doctors today have anesthesia that works much better than in the old days. They also have precise surgical tools and clean operating rooms. These measures make surgery much safer for patients today than it was long ago.

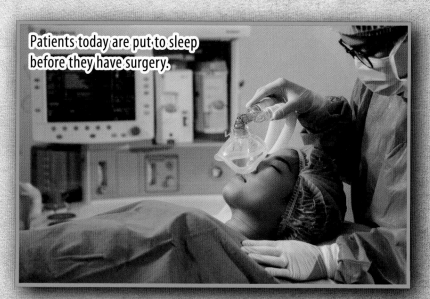

Patients today are put to sleep before they have surgery.

cauterize—to burn the skin or flesh of a wound with a hot tool or a chemical substance

anesthesia—a gas or injection that prevents pain during treatments and operations

Amputations

People sometimes have limbs removed due to accidents or disease. This is always upsetting for the patient. But in the past **amputations** were even more horrible. Sometimes there was no medicine to put patients to sleep during surgery so they would not feel the pain. Surgeons worked quickly to spare their patients pain.

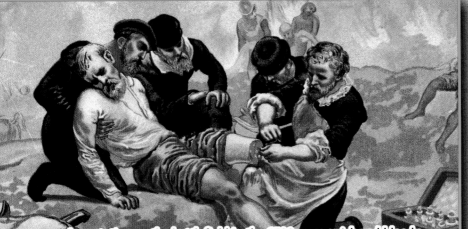

Amputation on the battlefield in the 1500s was quick and bloody.

BIZARRE FACT

During the Civil War (1861–1865) ether and chloroform were used in operations. However, these were not always available. Sometimes doctors had to amputate soldiers' arms and legs while the patients could feel everything!

amputation—the removal of an arm or a leg

Fastest Knife in Town

Sometimes surgeons worked too quickly. Scottish surgeon Robert Liston was called the "fastest knife in Edinburgh" in the 1800s. He was famous for his super-quick amputations. Some said he could remove an arm or leg in under 30 seconds!

Legend has it that one day Liston was in too much of a rush. He accidentally sliced off the fingers of his helper and slashed a spectator's coat. The spectator thought he had been stabbed. He died of shock. Both the patient and the helper died from infections.

Dr. Robert Liston performs surgery.

BIZARRE FACT

The first chainsaw was invented in Scotland— in the late 1700s. It was not used to cut trees, however. It was used to cut bones!

Eye Surgery

Cataracts in the eyes have always been a problem. The lens becomes cloudy. Eyesight gets blurry. Sometimes people go blind.

More than 1,000 years ago a surgeon in India had a solution. He used a curved needle to push the cloudy lens to the back of the eye. This made the patient's vision less blurry. After surgery the patient's eye was bathed with melted butter. Why butter? People believed that it would speed up recovery and help nourish the eye.

This modern drawing shows eye surgery in medieval India.

Modern surgery has made cataract removal quick, painless, and safe.

Later surgeons removed the cloudy lens from the eye. Medieval doctors in the Middle East performed this delicate surgery. They made a big cut in the patient's eye. Then they used a hollow needle to suck the cataract out through a straw. Eew!

Today cataract surgery is done using lasers. The laser breaks up the lens. Then the pieces are sucked out. A plastic lens is placed on the eye.

cataract—a condition in which the lens of the eye becomes cloudy

Treating Wounds

How did people treat wounds long ago? One Ancient Egyptian remedy used powdered ostrich egg to help dry out head wounds. Egyptian doctors also stuffed very deep wounds with honey or sugar. Some doctors in Germany use this technique today for seriously infected deep wounds. Sugar draws out water. So it helps keep the wound dry and promotes new tissue growth. And we now know that honey has **antiseptic** properties.

A leech can suck up five times its weight in blood in less than an hour.

BIZARRE FACT

Leeches have been used for many years for bloodletting. They are now being used to drain blood after surgery. They help heal the tissue by getting the blood flowing around the wound.

antiseptic—something that kills germs and prevents infection

In 2004 leeches and maggots became the first animals approved by the Food and Drug Administration as "medical devices."

MAGGOTS AS MEDICINE

Maggots are fly larvae. They are creepy. But believe it or not, they can help heal wounds! They have been used as medicine since Mayan times. Why? Maggots eat the dead skin of a wound. This helps to kill bacteria that can cause infection. Maggot saliva is also antiseptic.

Today's hospitals do not put just any old maggots into a patient's wound. They use specially bred ones delivered in sterile containers.

CHAPTER 4

TERRIFYING TREATMENTS

Bed rest is a recommended treatment for colds and flus.

Who hasn't caught a cold at some point? In the past treatments could be painful. Sometimes they tasted awful. And sometimes they were just bizarre.

Two thousand years ago the Romans thought demons caused sickness. So terrible things, such as eating rabbit poop, were prescribed to force out the cold demon.

Even today there are many folk remedies to treat the common cold. Some people in Hong Kong swear by lizard soup. The steam from the hot soup can help clear a person's air passages.

BIZARRE FACT

One remedy for the common cold in the 1700s was to spit constantly. People thought colds were caused by poisons in the air that mixed with saliva in the mouth.

Chinese lizard soup is made from dried lizards sold in Chinese medicine shops.

Lung Diseases

Diseases of the lungs have been around for thousands of years. Take **tuberculosis** (TB). TB is a deadly lung disease caused by bacteria.

More than 80 years ago there were no drugs to fight bacteria. Doctors would force plastic balls around a patient's lung. This caused the lung to collapse, giving it time to heal. Ouch!

BIZARRE FACT

Some Romans thought that winds caused TB. They tried to stop the spread of this illness by building walls. The walls were meant to block the "disease-causing" winds.

Inserting balls around the lungs was called "plombage." This X-ray shows the plastic balls.

plastic balls

Pneumonia

Another unpleasant lung ailment is **pneumonia**. This lung disease is also caused by bacteria. The lung becomes inflamed and full of fluid. One treatment for this disease was to remove one of the patient's ribs. This allowed doctors to get at the lung that needed draining. What a painful way to treat a disease!

THE CARBOLIC SMOKE BALL

The carbolic smoke ball was used in the 1800s. It was thought to help with many ailments of the head, throat, and lungs. A rubber ball was filled with powdered carbolic acid. The patient squeezed it. A puff of smoke would go up the nose. This was supposed to flush out the illness.

This advertisement for the carbolic smoke ball shows how it was used.

tuberculosis—an infectious bacterial disease affecting the lungs

pneumonia—a serious disease that causes the lungs to become inflamed and filled with a thick fluid that makes breathing difficult

The Bubonic Plague

Headaches, chills, and fever. A whitish-colored tongue. Black and purple spots on the skin. Swellings called buboes under the skin. Between the 1300s and 1600s the **bubonic plague** swept across Asia, Europe, and the Middle East. People now refer to this massive outbreak as the Black Death.

BIZARRE FACT

Drinking molten gold and powdered emeralds was said to be a remedy for the bubonic plague. But it was usually fatal—not to mention super-expensive!

Unusual Treatments for the Bubonic Plague

- bathing in urine
- drinking arsenic or mercury
- drinking melted gold and powdered emeralds
- strapping live chickens around the painful sores
- breathing in smoke and vinegar fumes
- using leeches in bloodletting

Experts say that as many as 200 million people died from the Black Plague.

Medicine-Then, Now, and in the Future

From Ancient Egypt to the present day, people have had many unusual ideas about medicine.

Why were many of these remedies so strange? Often no one knew what caused these health problems. People tried many folk remedies to recover from illness. A few of those treatments actually helped. Many others made matters worse. A lot of them just seem crazy to us today.

This computer artwork shows nanorobot surgery of the future.

What will medicine be like in the future? Will doctors be able to inject tiny robots into people's bodies to help cure them? And what do you think people of the future will think of today's medicine?

> **bubonic plague**—a deadly disease that causes high fevers, painful swelling of the lymph glands, and darkening of the skin; during the Middle Ages the plague was quickly spread by fleas that lived on rats

GLOSSARY

amputation (am-pyuh-TAY-shun)—the removal of an arm or a leg

anesthesia (a-nuhs-THEE-zhuh)—a gas or injection that prevents pain during treatments and operations

antiseptic (an-ti-SEP-tik)—something that kills germs and prevents infection

bloodletting (BLUHD LET-ing)—the act of letting out blood by opening a vein

bubonic plague (boo-BON-ik PLAYG)—a deadly disease that causes high fevers, painful swelling of the lymph glands, and darkening of the skin; during the Middle Ages the plague was quickly spread by fleas that lived on rats

cataract (KAT-ur-act)—a condition in which the lens of the eye becomes cloudy

cauterize (KAW-tur-ize)—to burn the skin or flesh of a wound with a hot tool or a chemical substance

constipation (kon-sti-PAY-shun)—difficulty having a bowel movement

enema (EN-uh-muh)—an injection of fluid that causes a bowel movement

epilepsy (E-puh-lep-see)—an illness that causes people to have blackouts or convulsions

pneumonia (noo-MOH-nyuh)—a serious disease that causes the lungs to become inflamed and filled with a thick fluid that makes breathing difficult

trepanning (tre-PAN-ning)—making a hole in a patient's skull, as with a hole saw called a trepan

tuberculosis (tu-BUR-kyoo-LOW-sis) an infectious bacterial disease affecting the lungs

READ MORE

Rooney, Anne. *The Story of Medicine.* The Story Of Series. London: Arcturus Publishing Limited, 2012.

Senior, Kathryn. *You Wouldn't Want to Be Sick in the 16th Century!: Diseases You'd Rather Not Catch.* New York: Children's Press, 2014.

Stefoff, Rebecca. *Magic and Medicine.* Is It Science? Series. New York: Cavendish Square Publishing, 2014.

Woods, Michael, and Mary B. Woods. *Ancient Medical Technology: From Herbs to Scalpels.* Technology in Ancient Cultures Series. Minneapolis: Twenty-First Century Books, 2011.

INTERNET SITES

FactHound offers a safe, fun way to find Internet sites related to this book. All of the sites on FactHound have been researched by our staff.

Here's all you do:

Visit *www.facthound.com*

Type in this code: 9781491442661

Check out projects, games, and lots more at **www.capstonekids.com**

INDEX